COOKING INNOVATIONS

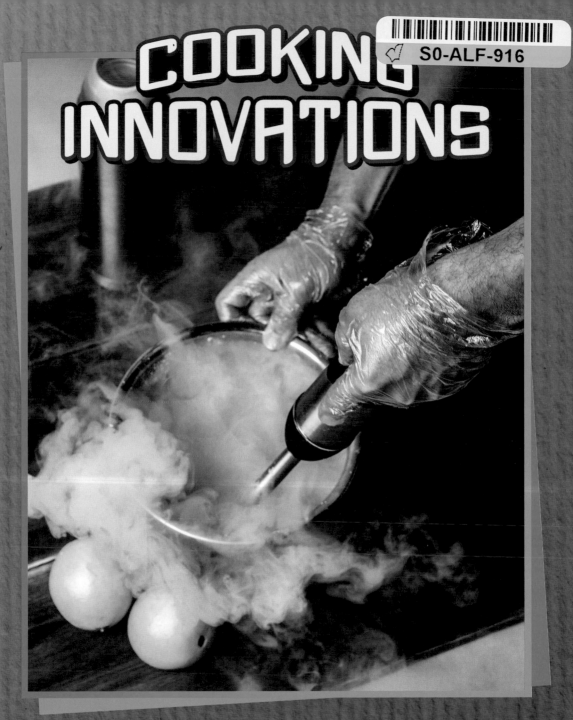

Lesley Ward

S0-ALF-916

✳ Smithsonian

© 2019 Smithsonian Institution. The name "Smithsonian" and the Smithsonian logo are registered trademarks owned by the Smithsonian Institution.

Contributing Author

Jennifer Lawson

Consultants

Ashley Rose Young, Ph.D.
Historian
American Food History
National Museum of American History

Sharon Banks
3rd Grade Teacher
Duncan Public Schools

Publishing Credits

Rachelle Cracchiolo, M.S.Ed., *Publisher*
Conni Medina, M.A.Ed., *Managing Editor*
Diana Kenney, M.A.Ed., NBCT, *Content Director*
Véronique Bos, *Creative Director*
Robin Erickson, *Art Director*
Michelle Jovin, M.A., *Associate Editor*
Mindy Duits, *Senior Graphic Designer*
Smithsonian Science Education Center

Image Credits: p.7 (bottom) Mauricio Anton/Science Source; p.8 Schenectady Museum Association/Getty Images; p.9 (left) Acroterion (Creative Commons); p.12 (left) Elizabeth/Table4Five (Creative Commons); p.13 Courtesy Pantelligent; p.14 (bottom) Courtesy PolyScience; p.15 (bottom) Makia Minich; p.22 First Class Photography/Shutterstock; p.23 Peter Titmuss/Alamy; p.24 (left) T. Tseng (Creative Commons); p.24 (right) Xabier Mikel Laburu/Bloomberg via Getty Images; p.25 (top) Lawrence K. Ho/Los Angeles Times via Getty Images; p.26 (bottom) Sam Bompas/Splash News/Newscom; pp.26–27 (top) Imagine China/Newscom; p.27 (bottom) PA Images/Alamy; all other images from iStock and/or Shutterstock.

Library of Congress Cataloging-in-Publication Data

Names: Ward, Lesley, author.
Title: Cooking innovations / Lesley Ward.
Description: Huntington Beach, CA : Teacher Created Materials, [2019] | Includes index. |
Identifiers: LCCN 2018031130 (print) | LCCN 2018032374 (ebook) | ISBN 9781493869114 (E-book) | ISBN 9781493866717 (pbk.)
Subjects: LCSH: Cooking--Technological innovations--Juvenile literature. | Cooking--History--Juvenile literature.
Classification: LCC TX652.5 (ebook) | LCC TX652.5 .W344 2019 (print) | DDC 641.509--dc23
LC record available at https://lccn.loc.gov/2018031130

☼ Smithsonian

© 2019 Smithsonian Institution. The name "Smithsonian" and the Smithsonian logo are registered trademarks owned by the Smithsonian Institution.

Teacher Created Materials

5301 Oceanus Drive
Huntington Beach, CA 92649-1030
www.tcmpub.com
ISBN 978-1-4938-6671-7

© 2019 Teacher Created Materials, Inc.
Printed in Malaysia
Thumbprints.21251

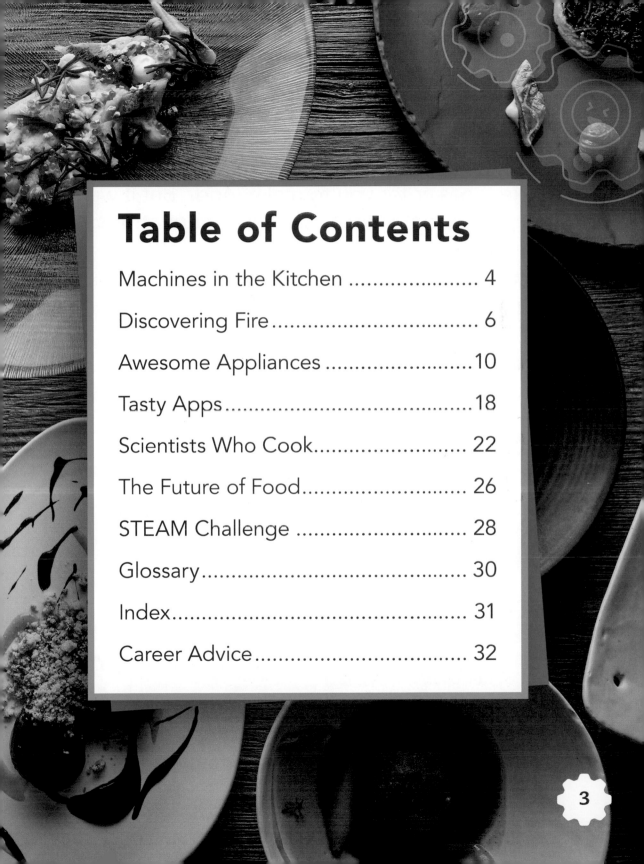

Table of Contents

Machines in the Kitchen

Look around your kitchen. It is home to some amazing machines. They are machines that help make it easier for you to make food. But it was not always that simple. Cooking **innovations** have come a long way. They often make our lives easier.

Chefs are thankful for these innovations. They use them to try new things. Chefs are scientists. Their kitchens are their laboratories. They try new ways to make food. Sometimes, they make something completely new!

This woman takes food out of her oven in the early 1900s.

4

Innovations like these can make cooking easier.

Discovering Fire

Before early humans learned how to make fire, their diets were much different. Early humans ate plants, fruit, and raw meat!

Many years later, humans started cooking their food. They might have used fires that were started by lightning. This was probably the first time humans ate cooked meat.

Over the years, humans learned to make their own fires. They learned how to keep fires burning for a long time. Families and friends ate around fires. Fire was their stove.

Some people still eat raw meat.

These chickens are being cooked over a campfire.

Early humans ate cooked plants.

People kept cooking with fire for thousands of years. In the 1890s, **electric** stoves were invented. These stoves made cooking faster and easier. There was no smoke and no ash. Plus, they helped keep homes warm. More and more people bought stoves. They were a hit.

In 1946, things changed again. An inventor named Percy Spencer was in his lab. He was studying radiation—a way heat travels. At one point, he reached down. His pocket was gooey. He realized radiation had melted his candy bar! Spencer learned he didn't need fire to cook. This led to the invention of the microwave.

A woman cooks on an electric stove.

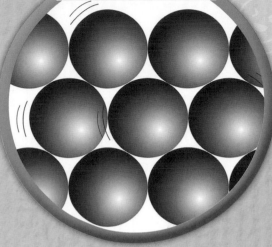

Molecules in cold solid foods are packed together.

This RadaRange was the first microwave and was as big as a refrigerator!

Molecules in heated solid foods move more freely.

How Microwaves Work

Microwaves heat **molecules** in food. All things are made of tiny molecules that you can't see. Microwaves send out energy. The energy causes molecules in food to vibrate. That movement makes heat. The heat cooks the food.

Awesome Appliances

Today, people do not have to work as hard to cook tasty meals. Most of that is due to new **appliances** that help them.

One new appliance is a radio frequency oven. This special oven helps people cook entire meals all at once. And it does it all very quickly. This helps keep **nutrients** in food.

Another new appliance is a hot-air fryer. It uses hot air to make food taste like it is deep-fried. The food is crisp on the outside. It is juicy on the inside. Many people like that the food is not greasy after it is cooked.

A hot-air fryer cooks chicken.

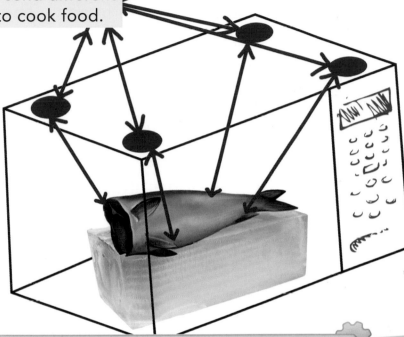

Radio Frequency Oven

Sensors send different beams to cook food.

Technology & Engineering

Oven Sensors

Radio frequency ovens have **sensors** in them. The sensors can tell what types of foods people are cooking. The ovens send different beams to cook each item. The sensors also scan the food every few seconds. They change the beams to give more or less heat. That way, meals finish at the same time.

Chefs try to make healthy, but tasty, foods. Some appliances help them do just that! Some pans have sensors that track what foods are in the pans. They tell people the right temperatures for cooking those foods. They make sure foods are cooked before people eat.

Chefs also try to find ways to save time when cooking. There are innovations to help there too. Some machines can bake cupcakes in just a few minutes. These machines heat from the top and the bottom at the same time. That means it takes much less time.

This cupcake maker bakes eight cupcakes in five minutes.

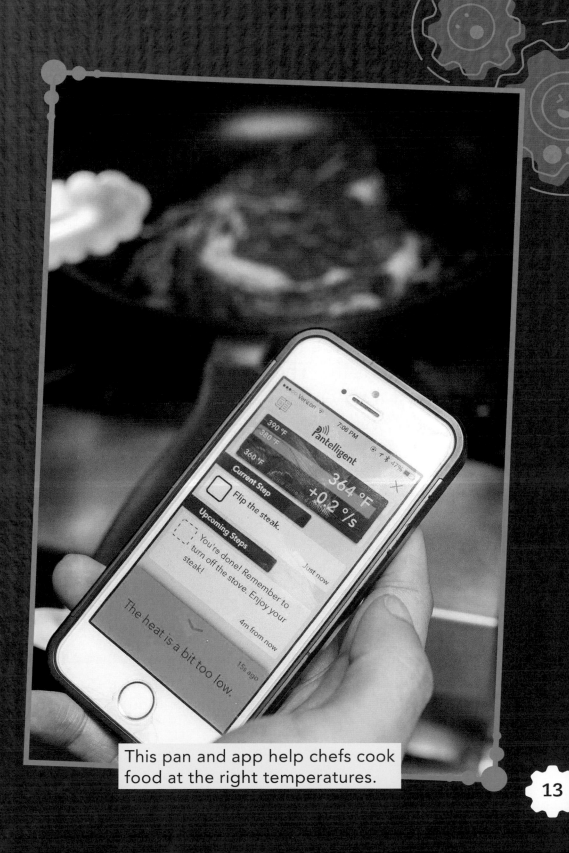

This pan and app help chefs cook food at the right temperatures.

Cool Chillers

Not all cooking innovations cook food. Some freeze food instead. Some machines can freeze liquids in under a minute. These machines have very cold trays on them. People can pour liquids onto the trays to make treats like frozen hot chocolate, frozen tea, and more. Then, they can grab a spoon and enjoy!

There are also machines that turn liquids into ice pops. First, chefs freeze the machine. Then, they pour liquids in. The machine freezes the liquids in just a few minutes. People can have orange juice pops. Or, maybe they want yogurt pops. The choice is theirs!

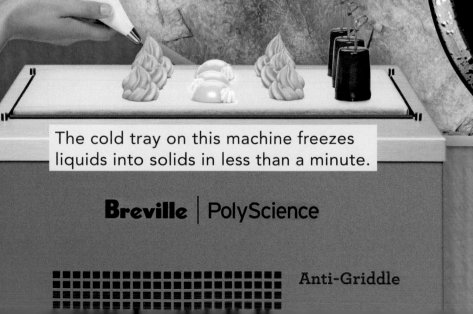

The cold tray on this machine freezes liquids into solids in less than a minute.

Breville | PolyScience

Anti-Griddle

This green tea ice cream was frozen from liquid tea.

This innovation can freeze any liquid into an ice pop in just a few minutes.

Another innovation comes from Thailand. Thailand has a lot of hot weather. Frozen foods melt quickly. So, chefs there found a new way to make ice cream.

This treat is called rolled ice cream. First, chefs pour milk onto a cold tray. Once it freezes, they scrape it off the tray. They roll it up carefully and put it in a cup. The best part? Since the ice cream is rolled up, it does not melt as quickly!

A chef in Thailand rolls ice cream.

Rolled ice cream can be made to taste like other foods, such as pretzels, pizza, and burgers!

Tasty Apps

Chefs do not just use machines to solve their cooking problems. They use apps too! Some apps have videos of famous chefs making meals. People can watch the videos as they cook their own foods. The chefs tell them what to do. It is like having a chef in your home!

There are also apps that have **recipes**. People can find meals that fit their lifestyles. If someone does not eat meat, there are recipes for them. Or, if someone wants a meal they can make quickly, there are recipes for them too. These apps make it easy for people to cook at home.

This app shows different recipes.

A man searches for dinner recipes while he eats breakfast.

This app shows pictures for each step of a recipe.

There are also apps that help people cook what they already have. People can enter the **ingredients** they have at home. The apps then search to find recipes that use those items. They tell people how to make meals with what they already have.

Other apps do the opposite. People enter the kinds of meals they like. Then, the apps tell them what ingredients to buy. People can share photos of their meals later. That helps other people when they cook.

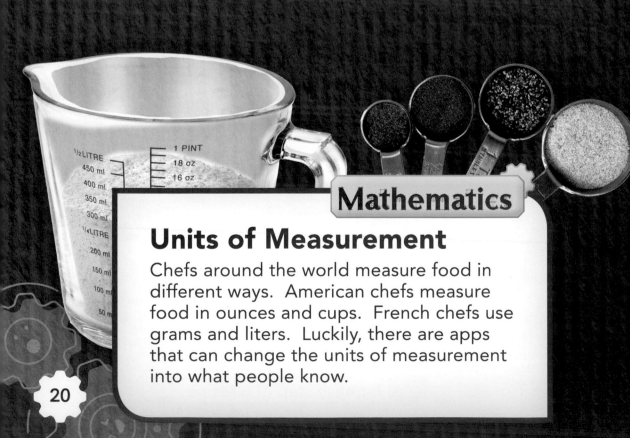

Mathematics

Units of Measurement

Chefs around the world measure food in different ways. American chefs measure food in ounces and cups. French chefs use grams and liters. Luckily, there are apps that can change the units of measurement into what people know.

Refrigerator

Shopping List

☑ Milk
☑ Meat
☑ Eggs
☑ Cheese
☐

A woman creates a shopping list based on what she has in her refrigerator.

This app shows what people need to buy to make a meal.

Scientists Who Cook

Chefs are scientists. They use tools and machines to experiment with food. Instead of labs, they run tests in kitchens and restaurants.

Chef Heston Blumenthal owns a restaurant in England called The Fat Duck. That is where he experiments. He uses liquid nitrogen to make ice cream that tastes like eggs and bacon. He also cooks beef with a **blowtorch**!

One of his meals is called Sound of the Sea. It is made of fish and seaweed. Sounds play as people eat. They hear waves. It makes people feel like they are at the beach!

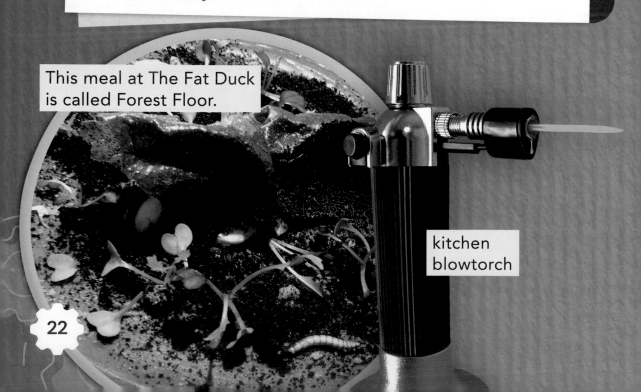

This meal at The Fat Duck is called Forest Floor.

kitchen blowtorch

Blumenthal experiments at The Fat Duck.

Ferran Adrià (feh-RAWN uh-dree-AH) lives in Spain. Some people say he is the world's best chef. He is famous for his foam foods.

Adrià mixes flavors with a special gel. Then, he adds gas. The gel turns into foam. Adrià sprays the foam onto plates. It may look unusual. But people think it is delicious!

Niki Nakayama (nah-kah-YAH-muh) is a chef who learned how to cook in Japan. Her meals have 13 parts. They can take a long time to eat!

Nakayama makes common food interesting. She serves salmon with water lilies. She also serves snails with potatoes. Her meals change. But they are always unusual!

Adrià in his restaurant

Nakayama makes sushi.

Framing Foods

American chef Lawrence Kocurek (kuh-SUHR-ihk) sees his food as art. He says that each plate is "a blank slate." He uses square plates because they are shaped like frames.

The Future of Food

Cooking innovations have made kitchens better than ever. Tools make it faster and easier to cook. People do not have to be **professional** chefs to make meals that taste good. All they need is to try something new.

What will the future of cooking hold? Who knows! The best way to find out is to experiment. Try something new, and see how it tastes. Keep trying until you find a cool new way to cook something. Then, share your recipe with friends. You can try new foods together. What will you bite into next?

A chef cooks steaks in seconds by using human-made lava.

A robot cooks a bowl of noodles in less than two minutes.

Some meat can be grown in labs instead of coming from animals.

STEAM CHALLENGE

Define the Problem

A chef has just moved to a new restaurant. But the new kitchen is smaller than she is used to. The chef has hired you to design a new tool for her. Your tool must be able to do multiple tasks to save space.

Constraints: Your tool must be made with no more than 10 items.

Criteria: Your tool must do two different kitchen tasks, such as stirring and flipping.

Research and Brainstorm

What are the most important tasks in the kitchen? Why should one tool be able to do multiple tasks?

Design and Build

Sketch a design of your tool. What purpose will each part serve? What materials will work best? Build the model.

Test and Improve

Test your tool. Was your tool able to perform both tasks? How can you improve it? Improve your design and try again.

Reflect and Share

What foods would your tool not work with? How could you change your tool for someone who normally could not do those tasks? How could you add technology to your tool?

Glossary

appliances—machines that are powered by electricity and can be used in homes

blowtorch—a tool that produces very hot, narrow flames

electric—operated by electricity

ingredients—things used to make foods

innovations—new ideas, methods, or devices

molecules—very small parts that make up all things

nutrients—things that plants, people, and animals need to live and grow

professional—refers to people who are specially trained and who get paid to do things

recipes—instructions for making food

sensors—devices that notice things

Index

Career Advice
from Smithsonian

Do you want to design tools for chefs? Here are some tips to get you started.

"Ask your family what they ate when they were kids. Make those same meals with tools you have now." —*Kathy Sklar, Business Program Manager*

"My mother and aunts taught me to appreciate foods from around the world. If you like to cook, think of what tools would make cooking easier. Then, make some!" —*Dr. Ashley Rose Young, Historian*